WARNING:

Too Much Schooling Can Damage Your Health

WARNING:

TOO MUCH SCHOOLING
CAN DAMAGE YOUR HEALTH

Trevor Millum

Nelson

ACKNOWLEDGEMENTS

The editor and publishers wish to thank the following who have kindly given permission for the use of copyright material:
Edward Arnold, a division of Hodder and Stoughton Limited, for the extract ' *In Bakerloo did Aly Khan...*' from **Considering Poetry** by B.A. Phythian.

Integrated Studies first appeared in **English in Education, Volume 20, No. 3.**

Thomas Nelson and Sons Ltd
Nelson House   Mayfield Road
Walton-on-Thames   Surrey
KT12 5PL   UK

© Trevor Millum 1988

Front cover illustration: **Mike Lamble**
All other illustrations: **Jo Wright**

First published by E J Arnold and Son Ltd 1988
ISBN 0-560-55016-2

This edition published by Thomas Nelson and Sons Ltd 1989
ISBN 0-17-432315-8
NPN 9 8 7 6 5 4

All rights reserved. No paragraph of this publication may be reproduced, copied or transmitted save with written permission or in accordance with the provisions of the Copyright, Design and Patents Act 1988, or under the terms of any licence permitting limited copying issued by the Copyright Licensing Agency, 90 Tottenham Court Road, London W1P 9HE.

Any person who does any unauthorised act in relation to this publication may be liable to criminal prosecution and civil claims for damages.

Printed in China.

CONTENTS

A NOTE TO TEACHERS   8

EARLY MORNING   12

The Raid of the Head-Bangers   13
Bell Rings   14
Guarantee   15
Paper Round   16
Junk Mail   18
It Isn't Fair   19
Trousers is a Silly Name   20
Head Cold   21

OFF TO SCHOOL   22

Bad News   23
Timetable   24
What It All Means   25
Exploding Heads (1)   26
Istri   28
Chemistry   30
There's More Than One Way of Skinning Some Art   31
Fill In Your Own Weather Poem   32
If I Was a Frog   33
Exam   34

BREAK   36

The Fags on Which They Drag   37
E322 — or Is My Mother Trying to Kill Me?   38
The Summons   40
Fighting Fantasy   41
Integrated Studies   42

Duet	44
Cheap OAPs	47
Headline	47
Jane Johnson - Infinitely Bored	48
Graffiti	49

JUST CONCENTRATE   50

Pupils and Teachers — Peculiar Creatures	51
I Really Tried . . . But I Couldn't Help It	52
Mr Taylor's All Right	54
Teacher Giving Orders	55
Teacher	56
New Teacher, Old Class	57
Just Concentrate	58
Testing Testing 123 Testing	59
Jabbermockery	60
Ten Little Schoolchildren	62
Exploding Heads (2)	64
The Head Boy's Refrain	65

THE EVENING SHIFT   66

What Did You Do at School Today, Dear?	67
The Evening Shift	68
The Song of the Homeworkers	69
Swap? Sell? Small Ads Sell Fast	70
Standing On My Head	71
Plug Her In or	
How to Deal With an Almost Adult Sister	72
Younger Brother	74
Alone in the House	75

DREAMS AND MEMORIES 76

I Dreamt I Took Over My Secondary School 77
A Glimpse 78
Deferred Gratifications 79
Caught Short, A Dream 80
The Jungle Sale . . . Another Dream 82
Embarrassing Memories from the Playground 84
Sad I Ams 86
Picture Poems 88
Fragments Overheard . . . 91

ESCAPE 92

Don't Pick It 93
On Yer Bike 94
The Power of Positive Thinking 98
Theatre Trip 100
Leaving School Blues 103

IDEAS FOR WRITING 107

A NOTE TO TEACHERS
(and anyone else who wants to read it)

This is a book of poems which were written for fun, together with some ideas for writing. It's not a poetry-writing handbook, which I think works the other way around. There are several very good such books, which I'll list at the end in case you haven't come across them.

The book grew slowly and only gradually assumed its present form. The poems were written over a long period: about seven or eight years. When I found that I had about twenty I made them into a booklet and used them with my pupils. When the booklets got tatty and needed replacing I put another collection together and discovered that the number of poems had doubled. And so it went on until I had enough to form a small book. It was only then that I thought it might be useful to include some of the ideas I had been using for teaching in case other people found them helpful too. So the poems have very definitely come first.

I wrote the poems for fun — or at least for pleasure — and pupils read them for fun. That is still the aim. Of course, it's true that poetry isn't always fun (and certainly isn't always funny) but I make no apologies for stressing this aspect. I think most, if not all, of the things that I now appreciate *seriously* started out as fun: drama, writing, music, art — even things as diverse as cricket and the protection of the environment. And as we all know, there's many a true word spoken in jest . . .

There isn't really a particular age group at which the poems are aimed. Top juniors have enjoyed them and so have school-leavers — obviously they get different things out of them! If I had to place this book in a *year* I think I would compromise and use it with third year pupils (13-14 year olds) because there's often a gap there which can be hard to fill.

Hopefully, readers will discover that there's a lot of fun to be had from writing as well. In both sections it is variety and choice which are the keynotes. Pupils will choose which poems they want to read again or to read out loud. Teachers and pupils will come up with starting points for their own writing. Some will work well, some will be abandoned. If a reader achieves three of four poems which he or she is glad to have written, the *Ideas For Writing* section will have served its purpose well.

I recommend these books to teacher and pupil alike:

Does It Have To Rhyme?	Sandy Brownjohn **Hodder & Stoughton**
Writing Poems	Harrison and Stuart-Clark **Oxford**
I See A Voice	Michael Rosen **Hutchinson**
Poetry in the Making	Ted Hughes **Faber**
Start-Write	Ed. Morag Styles **E.A.R.O.**

TREVOR MILLUM

For Danny and Joe

EARLY MORNING

The Raid of the Head-Bangers

Psst!
This way —
Through 'ere.
Quiet . . .
'E's still asleep, 'e won't notice.
Down this passageway
Up through that trapdoor
Careful . . .
Right: start by undoin' them screws,
That's it —
Prise the edges loose . . .
'Ey you, Gremlin,
Tap on that side
Wiv this mallet
Gently!
Good, good. Keep knocking
While I jump up and down
On the floor.
OK: switch on the light,
Wammo, start heaving bricks
At the wall and
Give the brain a good shake
So it proper wobbles about,
Make sure 'e's really awake . . .
Now — get the hammer-drills out!

Mum! Oooh . . . ouch . . .
*I've got a **dreadful** headache!*

BELL RINGS

*The purpose of education is
to develop a lively and
enquiring mind . . .*

ALARM RINGS YOU RISE
VOICE CALLS YOU EAT
RADIO GIVES TIME YOU LEAVE
DIESEL POWERED VEHICLE ARRIVES YOU BOARD
VEHICLE HALTS YOU WALK
BELL RINGS YOU SIT
YOUR NAME IS CALLED YOU SPEAK
BELL RINGS YOU MOVE
BELL RINGS YOU MOVE
BELL RINGS YOU SALIVATE YOU EAT
BELL RINGS YOU SIT
BELL RINGS YOU STAND
BELL RINGS YOU JUMP
BELL RINGS RINGS RINGS
YOU QUEUE
VEHICLE HALTS YOU BOARD
IT STOPS YOU WALK
VOICE SPEAKS YOU ANSWER
VOICE SHOUTS YOU EAT
TRANSISTOR SINGS YOU LISTEN
VIDEO CALLS YOU WATCH
TV SAYS TIME YOU LEAVE
SET CLOCK
IT TICKS YOU SLEEP
AND DREAM YOU REALLY NOT MACHINE

Guarantee

We want you to enjoy
The contents of this packet
If the cereal
Is not in perfect condition
Please return
The packet and contents
Stating if possible
When and where
It was bought.

We want you to enjoy
The contents of this lesson
If the teacher
Is not in perfect condition
Please return
The lesson and contents
Stating if possible
When and where
It was taught.

I want me to enjoy
The contents of this daydream
If the fantasy
Is not in perfect condition
I will return
The daydream and its contents
Stating why
When and where
It was thought.

Paper Round

1 . . . **2** . . .
Mirror for you
3 . . . woof . . . **4** . . .
Dog behind the door
5 . . . **6** . . .
Latch that sticks
7 . . . **8** . . .
Rotten gate
9 . . . **10** . . .
Extra comics again!
11 . . . **12** . . . and over the road to **13** . . .
That kid's always watching behind the curtain
14 . . . ouch! . . . **15** . . .
These bikes want shifting
16 . . . **17** . . . **18** . . .
That bloke in pyjamas is always waiting
19 . . . **20** . . .
Still got plenty
21 . . . **22** . . . **23** . . .
Letter box much too low for me
24 . . . crunch crunch . . . **25** . . .
Helluva walk down their gravel drive
Hop over the hedge and round to **30**
Hands already filthy dirty
Across the street to **31**
Might've known they'd have the *Sun*
Just one more and then that's that:
Done the easy bit —
Now the Flats!

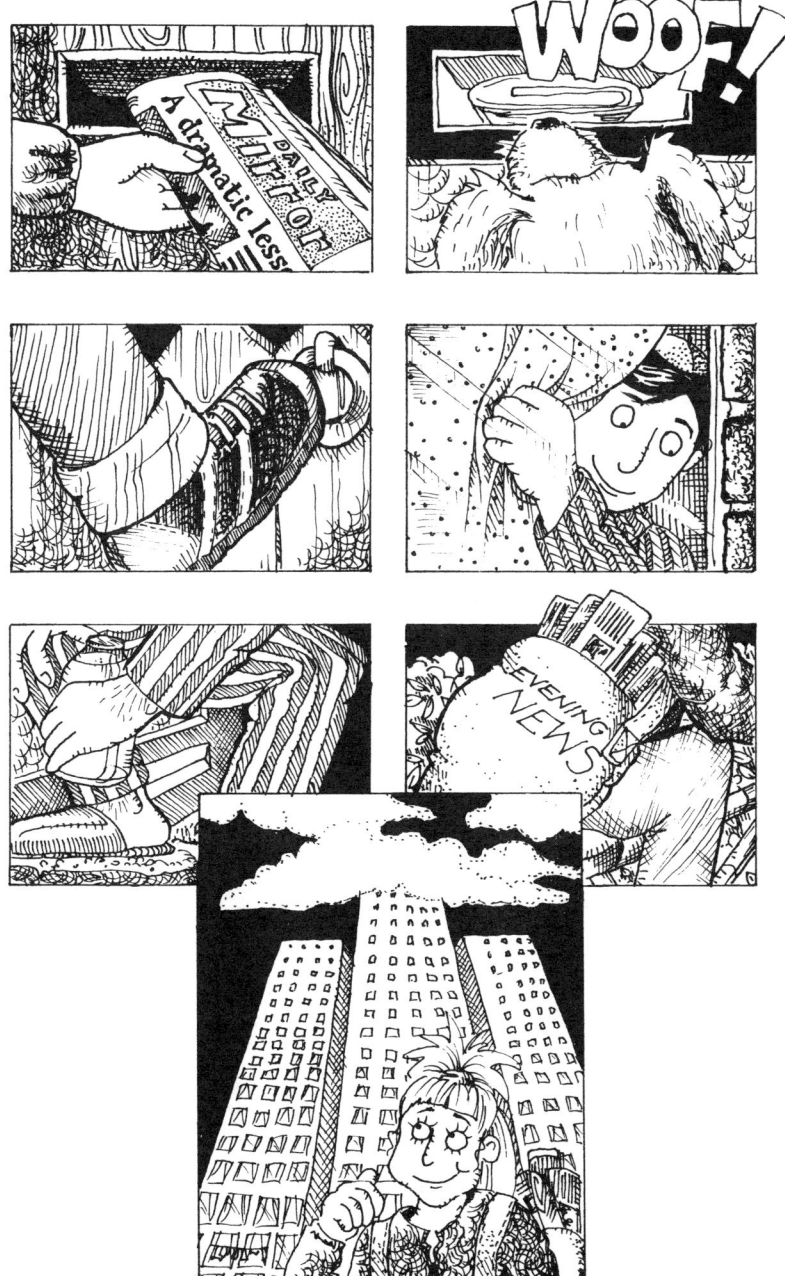

Junk Mail

It flaps through the door
Looking nice and fat,
Yes, it lands on the floor
And lies on the mat.
You rush to see who's written —
Argh! It's only more
Chorus: *JUNK MAIL!*
JUNK MAIL, JUNK MAIL,
IT'S JUST JUNK MAIL!

Mail order catalogues
Specially for you,
You're a valued customer,
Order twenty-two!
Take advantage of our offer
Too good to be true
In your . . . *JUNK MAIL!*

You're the lucky winner
Of a lucky digit draw;
All the lucky people
Can be really lucky sure
That their lucky number
Will leave them with some more . . .
JUNK MAIL!

Is your house insured?
Burglars can be rough!
Do you have the cover
For when things get tough?
We've a special plan
To ensure you get enough . . .
JUNK MAIL!

It Isn't Fair

I never get the comfy chair
Never get a say
In how I want my hair
Never get the extra pudding
When there's some to spare
Never get a choice
In what I want to wear!
Sometimes I wonder
If it's just that
They don't care
About their only
Cute and cuddly
Cat!

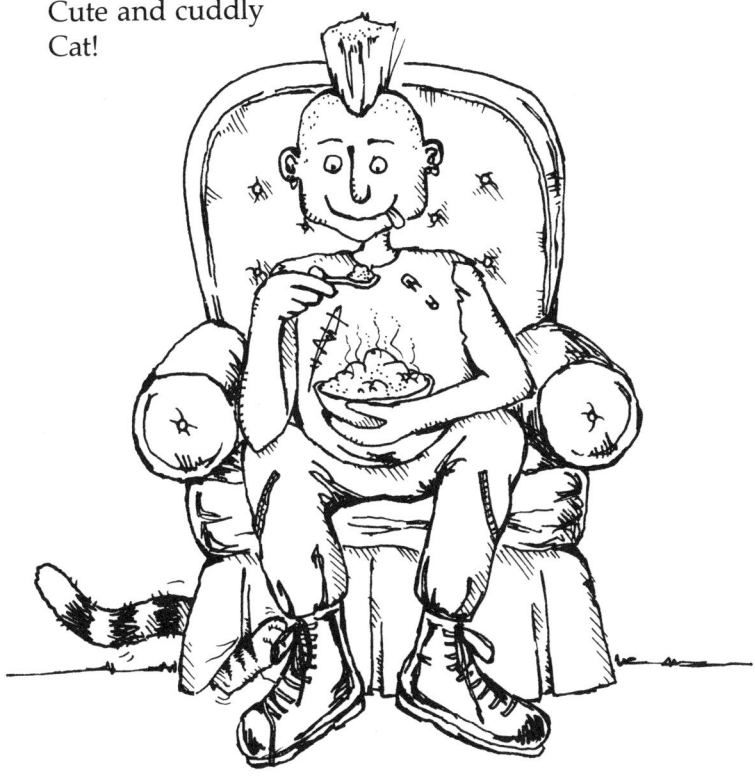

Trousers is a Silly Name

Like scissors:
A silly things
They is.
Always talking
Like there's
Two of it —
Or more!
(*And flies . . .*
Who thought up
That . . . or those?!)
I'm off to put on
  my new trouser;
Or shall I wear
  my jean?
  my short?
  my trunk?
The fact that I've
  two legs
  are no excuses;
I've got
  two arm
But I don't put on
  my shirts
  each days.

Trousers is
A silly name.
But we call our dog it
Just the same.
Is that why he eats
Enough for two??

Head Cold

Like Mum's car this morning
MY BRAIN WON'T GO:
Whirr-rum-rum . . . rum . . .
Our old lawn mower
Has a cord you tug
That sparks the sparking plug:
Whirr-rum-rumrumrumrum!
Wish I had one,
Going through my head;
Just pull it from my ear,
THEN the ideas will start.
Whirr-rum-rum . . . rum . . .?
However hard I try
I still won't go.
How about a push start, Miss,
Some jump leads — or a tow?

OFF TO SCHOOL

Bad News

I knew it was no good
The day that letter came
For me dad
                    (*bad news*)

He gave me a speech
On how much better school was
Than when he was a lad
                    (*how does he know?*)

They gave me a timetable
It looked like a maths problem
Gone mad
                    (*a Brainiac made it*)

They gave me a form teacher
Who looked frightened, bewildered
And sad
                    (*hoping for early retirement*)

They gave me a sort of dinner
And the jam roly-poly wasn't
Too bad
                    (*the custard was cold*)

They gave me some — lessons
I think they called them:
Made us glad
                    (*when the bell went*)

They're gonna give me an *All Round Education*
And prepare me for *Life* . . .
Ever been had?

Timetable

Period 1 and period 2: Mathematics in 52;
Period 3: Geography in Room 40 B;
English with Smudger for Period 4;
R.E. in 20, that's next door;
Science for a double in Lab Number 9;
History in 30 is the end of the line.
Lots of minutes for learning, few for play:
How educated I'll be by the end of the day!

(*Do I have to go again tomorrow?*)

What It All Means

*An explanation of the
traditional curriculum
in terms we can all
un-der-stand.*

Today we've got History
The story of hissing
Then we've got Physics
The science of fizzing
Later is Geography
The way to go jogging
Then we've got Mew-sic
The language of moggies
Tomorrow there's Science
The study of sighing . . .
My favourite's Biology
The science of buying
And then there is Art
About beating and being
And finally P.E.
The time to be —
Keeping your mouth shut.

Exploding Heads (1)

Did I tell you about the day the Head exploded?
    He was up on the stage
    In his usual way
    Hands clasped together
    About to say, *Let us pray* . . .
    When all of a sudden
    Don't know what was the matter
    He went quite berserk
    And grew fatter and fatter . . .

Everyone looked up, their attention riveted on the expanding figure in front of them.
    He *was* in a state —
    In a terrible tizz,
    His eyes were rotating
    And his tongue it went fizz,
    His knees started knocking:
    Made a terrible row
    And then he blew up
    With a furious Ka-POW!

Well, you can imagine the mess it made.
> There were bits of his liver
> In the rissoles that day
> And we found both his knees
> When we went out to play.
> Sparrows flew off
> With toes in their beaks
> And bits I won't mention
> Were collected for weeks.

The Deputy looked a bit taken aback by this
unforeseen alteration to the day's timetable . . .
> She tried to think quickly
> Of a suitable hymn
> As she looked at the place
> Where the Head had just been
> "Now, school, we'll sing number
> One hundred and seven:
> *For All of Thy Blessings
> We Thank Thee, O Heaven.*"

Istri

I like istri
Think I know why
I like maps
And battle plans
Arrows to show
Angles, Jutes and Danes
Family trees
With the longest reigns
Diagrams of Viking ships
And coloured lines
For Columbus's trips
But most of all
. . . I like the names!
Not ones like
William
Henry
Charles
or James . . .
BUT

Theodoric the Ostrogoth, Tamburlaine the Great,

Stilicho the Vandal, Vladivostock, The Palatinate,

Sarmatians, Sumerians, Saracens, Silesians,

Venezuelans, Varangians, Voroshilov and Venetians,

Ivan the Terrible, Arthur the Awful,

Ethelred the Unready and Aelric the Unlawful!

can damage your health

(pause for breath)

Oh, I like istri
Think I know why
I like maps
And battle plans
Arrows to show
Angles, Jutes and Danes
Family trees
With the longest reigns
Diagrams of Viking ships
And coloured lines
For Columbus's trips
But most of all
I like the NAMES!
NOT ones like
William
Henry
Charles
or James
BUT
    Transylvania   Transcaucasia
           Transiberia   Tripolitania
    Hammurabi   Ashurbanipal
          Ras Sharma   and   Rumania
    Mzilikazi   Shaka Zulu
          Dingiswayo   Boadicea
    Heracleopolis   Alexandroupolis
          Chandragupta   Laodicea
    Hispaniola   Martinique
          Trinidad   and   Tobago
BARBAROSSA
        ZARAGOSSA
              TENOCHTITLAN
and *TIERRA*
        del
            FUEGO !!!

Chemistry

There's bromine in that jar. It leaks away
However tight you turn the top.
However tight, the vapour will not stay
Inside. It creeps, it seeps,
It even turns the screw top lid
And makes its nasty presence felt.

There's thoughts like that inside me, pushing out;
Please, Teacher, just twist the top on extra tight
And clamp me down and then I'll be all right.

There's More Than One Way of Skinning Some Art

I'm no good at Art . . .
But anyway,
One day
I was at home
With pens and blank paper
When the cat jumped up.
I was at the table by the window
So I wasn't surprised:
She liked to look out at the bins.
But she left behind
Five brown-grey prints of paws,
(Don't ask why five)
And without thinking
I coloured in some claws
Drew outlines
Stalks and leaves
And gave it in.
Marvellous, said Sunshine
Our smiling Art teacher,
You've really got it!
I told the cat
But she looked disbelieving
And turned up her tail.
I thought I might invite
Her to stand upon my Maths book
But decided not.
No sense in pushing your luck.

                                            R. Twerk

Fill In Your Own Weather Poem

The weather in my English book:
    Thick clouds of words
    Isolated outbreaks of full stops
    And scattered commas.

And later:
    Thick clouds of red remarks
    Isolated outbreaks of ticks
    And scattered exclamation marks!

The weather on my teacher's face:
    Thick clouds of information
    Isolated outbreaks of shouts and threats
    And scattered smiles.

The weather ....
    Thick clouds ....
    Isolated outbreaks of............................
    And scattered ....

If I Was a Frog

If I was a frog, I'd hop
Out of the chair — and some people would scream;
If I was a jelly fish, I'd flop
On the floor — and when someone trod on me
They'd slide across the room
And land with a clump on their backside;
If I was an albatross, I'd flap
My wings and look knowingly
As people fled outside;
If I was a seal, I'd clap
My flippers and look shiny, cute and cool
As people smiled and wished
They could have a miniature one of me
In their fishpond or paddling pool . . .
But as I'm human:
The most advanced species
Ever to hop or flop, flap or spring
Across the face of the earth,
I'll just sit here waiting for the bell to ring.

Exam

Heads down in rows
Pens ready, let's go.
Question 1, Question 2
Will any order do?
X has his hand under his chin,
Y has his to his brow
and Z leans on one elbow.
Q is yawning now
Pen between teeth
Plastic to enamel
His feet twisted beneath
The too small desk.
J gapes grimly at
Another page:
Answer two from Section B
And do from Section C
Any three not covered, they say,
In Sections B or A;
I'll do Question 7 anyway.

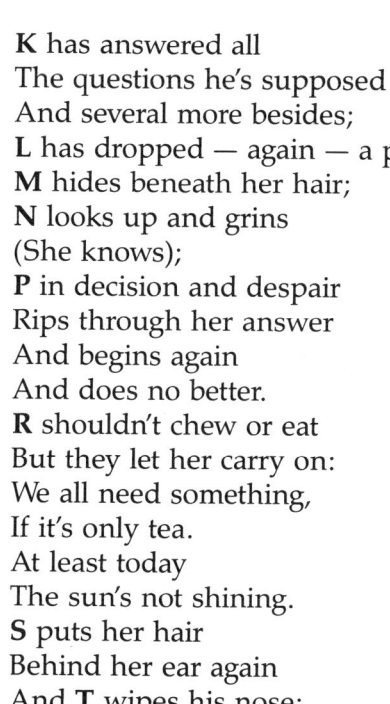

K has answered all
The questions he's supposed to
And several more besides;
L has dropped — again — a pencil;
M hides beneath her hair;
N looks up and grins
(She knows);
P in decision and despair
Rips through her answer
And begins again
And does no better.
R shouldn't chew or eat
But they let her carry on:
We all need something,
If it's only tea.
At least today
The sun's not shining.
S puts her hair
Behind her ear again
And **T** wipes his nose;
He knows he's only passing time
Until the buzzer goes.

BREAK

The Fags on Which They Drag

There's one secret smoker
In the bogs at break
Says the fags on which she drags
Are keeping her awake.

There's two secret smokers
By the sheds at dinner
Say the fags on which they drag
Help to keep them thinner.

There's three secret smokers
During Art & Craft
Say the fags on which they drag
Save them going daft.

There's four swaggering smokers
Going home from school
Feel the fags on which they drag
Will show that they're no fools.

There's five desperate smokers
In the staffroom after lessons
Wish the fags
On which they drag
Had never
Been
Invented!

E322-
or Is My Mother Trying to Kill Me?

I don't have school dinners:
My mum packs up a box,
So I scoff my sarnies in the Hall —
Watch the others getting spots.
I have brown bread with bits in
Spread with soya marg and cheese,
I just stare at chips and custard,
The batter and the peas . . .
I get a balanced diet
Don't stuff myself with starch,
Protect my teeth from sugar,
Keep them strong and sharp.

But today she put a biscuit
In with all my grub,
A chocolate covered biscuit:
A symbol of her love.
I idly read the packet
Saw what they'd put inside.
I read the wrapper once again
And then I nearly died!

There's emulsifier E322,
the sugar and the flour,
whey powder, glucose syrup,
colouring (110, 102, 150) & some malt,
cocoa (fat reduced),
milk chocolate flavouring
— would you believe? —
antioxidant 320
and a bit of bleeding salt!

I read it through just one more time,
I gulped, and then I thought:

SHE'S TRYING TO KILL ME!

But I ate it anyway and I'm not d_e_a_d _y _e _t.

The Summons

I was sent for
So I went, for
You must go
When you are sent for.

I stood outside, Sir,
The Deputy's door, Sir,
And studied carefully
The corridor floor, Sir.

And then, *Come in, John.*
So in I went.
*You needn't look, John,
So innocent!*

I changed my face, then,
I tried my best, then,
So I could look as
Guilty as the rest, and . . .

*Ah, now I see, John,
It's written clearly on
Your young face and
You'll pay dearly, John!*

I confess all, Sir,
And all I ask, Sir,
Is that next time
I can wear a mask — Sir!

Fighting Fantasy

The princes
are all dead
or old;
the castles
have been sold
to property developers . . .
There's been no duels
for ages;
the dragons
are all in cages
and the knights
have proper jobs
or futures in showbiz . . .
So, maiden,
looking to the distant blue,
who do you think
is going
to rescue
YOU?

Integrated Studies

On the front of his
Integrated Science Note Book
Were the names
Of all the motorcycles
He could think of.
His favourite was
KAWASAKI
It sounded best and
Looked good written in red.

On the front of her
Child Care and Cookery Note Book
Were the names
Of some of the singers
She liked at the time.
Her favourite was
ELVIS PRESLEY
Because he was dead.

For months they ignored
Each other's choice of names.
Motorbikes are just toys
For big boys to play games,
She thought. He thought
Singers were just noise
To stop you being bored.

Now I notice
He's added a guitar
To the emblems of bikes,
While she's added wheels
To the things that she likes.

And she's drawn a new sign
(On her new book) with some pride:
A heart with **Sue 4 John**
Neatly written inside.
But John hasn't drawn
A heart on his petrol tank.
I wonder if there's anything in it?

Duet

Once upon a time
   last week

In a dark dank castle yard
   our playground

Stood a modest misty-eyed maiden
   our Vicky

In the grip of a scaly spotted serpent
   Wayne Smith

And its oily orc-like allies.
   Ian and Alan

The valiant virile warrior
   me

Strode straight through the mighty portal
   the school gates

Bearing his sharp and shiny sword and dagger
   compass and ruler

And roaring, "Avaunt ye miscreants and malefactors!"
   Oi you!

"Unhand yon pure and matchless maid upon the instant!"
   Geroff our Vicky

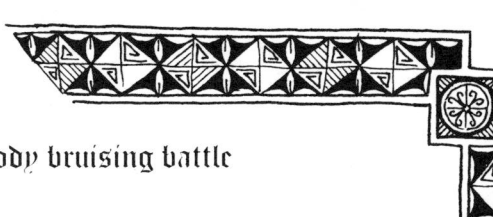

𝕿here ensued a bloody bruising battle
   a big scrap

𝖂hich will be remembered in the great tales of heroic deeds;
   till next week

𝕭ut then the clamorous din diminished
   it went quiet

𝕬nd they cowered in the shadow of an even mightier and more menacing monster
   the Head

𝖂hose nostrils breathed forth fire and eyes flashed most fearsome.
   he was not pleased

𝕴ncarcerated in a grim and gloomy dungeon
   his office

𝕿he warrior was fearless in his just denunciations of the evil trio;
   I blamed them

"𝕴 saved her from their low and loathsome clutches," quoth he.
   I showed off

𝕿he monstrous fire-breathing eye-flashing form demandeth, "𝕭e there yet truth in this, O damsel?"
   is he right?

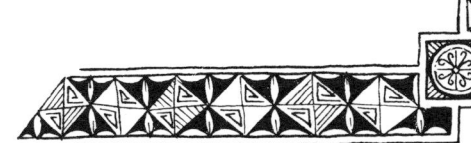

𝕿he warrior lifted his noble head proudly; he would be not merely saved, but honoured!
 I was confident

Quoth she, "Not one jot, O noble lord."
 NO
 eh?

And declared in roundest terms the scaly spotted serpent was her beloved!
 Wayne Smith was her boyfriend!

𝕿he warrior was wan, discomfitted, forlorn . . .
 I was fed up

And swore an awesome, mouth-filling, teeth-grinding, toe-curling oath to be avenged!
 just wait till our mum
 hears about this!!!

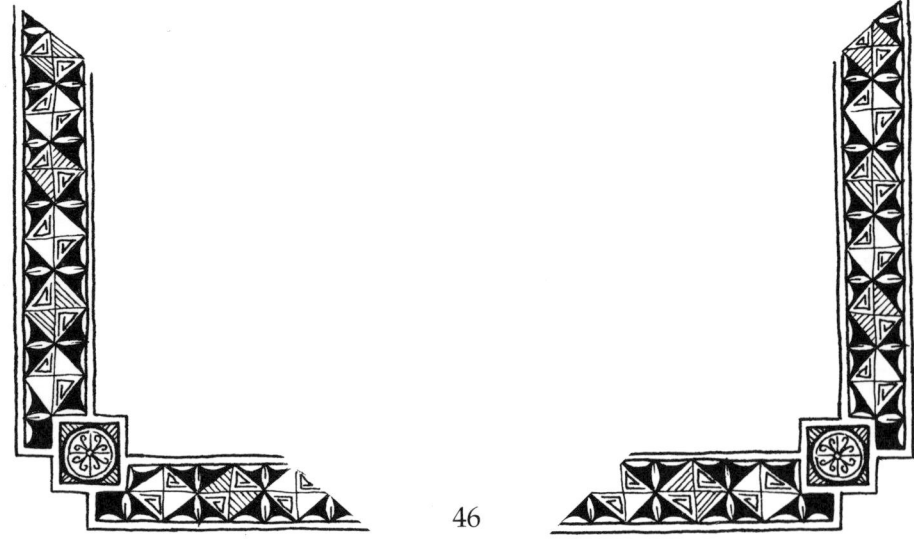

Cheap OAPs

The sign in the High Street
Chip Shop clearly said
OAPS 20% OFF
I thought maybe I'd buy one
For me grandad;
He's been lonely since
Me nan died
And it'd be nice
For there to be
Someone else about the plaice.

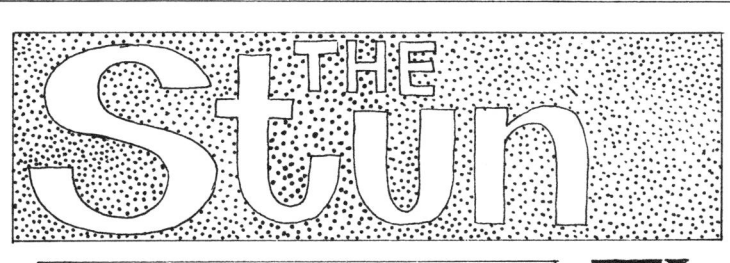

HEAD SAYS YES TO TOPLESS PREFECTS

A prefect (interviewed
Behind a high brick wall):
Who cares who stares?
I can clear the corridors
By standing in the Hall.

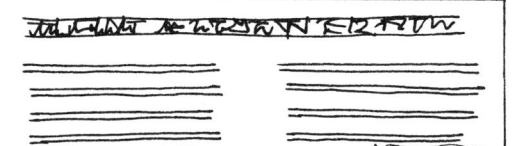

Jane Johnson, Infinitely Bored

Jane Johnson — she's the one
Round faced and large eyed,
Like a bush baby
Shaved and surprised . . .
But infinitely bored.
The most gripping thriller,
Most stirring romance,
Mouth-opening blood and thunder:
She rolls her eyes to the ceiling
As if to say why bother
To even open the cover,
It's only words again.
Infinitely bored.
Life has failed to reach her.
Somewhere the spark is missing,
The blood in her veins diluted
With rose-petal nail varnish,
The grey cells mixed with Weetabix.
Infinitely bored.
In a passionate embrace
With her fifth form boyfriend
She stifles a yawn
Or doesn't bother to stifle it
Or doesn't even yawn:
Even yawning gets boring.
Infinitely boring,
Jane Johnson.
She can function well enough
In mechanical situations
Yet let no one
Have expectations
Of life to come . . .

Somewhere something
Was earthed too soon
The vital power drained out
And left her
Infinitely bored.

Graffiti

The notes are unintelligible

The writing's quite illegible

The teacher's like a vegetable

But you're OK.

JUST CONCENTRATE

Pupils and Teachers
Peculiar Creatures

Pupils and teachers:
Peculiar creatures;
Animal, human, legend or fact?
Hunters or hunted?
Predators or prey?
Hear how they snarl
In much the same way;
Look at their features
From the same clay;
Animal, human, legend or fact?
Peculiar creatures:
Pupils and teachers.

I Really Tried . . . But I Couldn't Help It.

I really tried, Miss
To find my book
I got me brother
To help me look.
>He looked up in the airing cupboard
>and down in the dog basket
>and even in the breadbin
>but he couldn't find it.

I really tried, Sir
To do that stuff
My dad he said
It was really tough.
>He tried adding it up upwards
>and dividing it down downwards
>and even timesing it sideways
>but he couldn't do it.

I really tried, Miss
To keep it neat
But the dog got on it
With its muddy feet.
>It wandered from side to side
>and crossed from corner to corner
>and even sat in the middle
>but it didn't realise.

I really tried, Sir
To bring it in
But my book got put
In the washing machine.
    It lathered it this way
    and lathered it that
    and even rinsed it really clean
    but it didn't spin dry.

The teacher tried
To keep calm and cool
Because violence has
No place in school
And we must learn
To keep control.
He knew he shouldn't pick him up by the ears
Swing him sideways
And fling him downstairs
He really tried!
But he couldn't help it.

Mr Taylor's All Right

He's always cracking corny jokes —
He's a sort of *I'll-have-no-nonsense* bloke,
Who wouldn't tell you not to smoke:
Just take your fags until tomorrow
And when he gives them back, *I'm sorry*
That they're not all there, I had to borrow
One or two — or three or four. Hope you don't mind
— Who's keeping score?
He doesn't tend to get upset
Doesn't nag or moan or fret
About your clothes or hair, or let
Your chewing get him down . . .
BUT if you think you'll clown
Around — THEN you'll see the famous frown
And that ominous growling sound
As if a bomb's about to drop
Or the doodlebug's drone has cut — and stopped
AND SOMEONE'S GOING TO COP THE LOT!
But as long as it's not
You whose face is grimly turning white,
Mr Taylor . . . he's all right.

Teacher Giving Orders

I'd like to place an order
(If they're still for sale)
Two dozen pupils, various sizes,
Say, 13 female and 11 male.

No one ugly, no one too refined,
All with simple names that rhyme,
Clear complexions, no bad breath:
You know, the sort that give their
        Homework in on time.

(What do you mean, there's no more in stock?)

Teacher

He knows the game;
His expression, his voice
Exert his will. His posture
Leaves no choice
But to be silent.
With the boot of his command
He steps upon their chatter
Not to cajole but to demand
The ceasing of their babble.
His tone, his act, they understand.

New Teacher, Old Class

**Teacher
chalking**

Pupil One	Two	Three	Four
talking	talking	talking	talking
Five	Six	many	more

**Teacher
shouting**

Pupil One	Two	Three	Four
chalking	quiet	quiet	talking
Five	Six	Seven	Eight
throwing	flicking	blowing	clouting

**Teacher
glowing**

Pupil One	Two	Three	Four
shouting	chalking	talking	walking
Five	Six	Seven	Eight
eating	spitting	greeting	going

Teacher . . . .
. . . . **gone**

Just Concentrate!

The pen, to borrow or to find, takes time.
What's the title, Sir? Now underline.

Start . . . stop. Cross out. Begin again.
Look at the wall and tap the pen;
Write a line too rapidly — and then

Stare at the empty side: the uncommitted crime.
And at the bottom — there at the paper's edge —
A damp patch gathers. At some later stage

The hand, now tacky, sticks onto the sheet.
It's moved — somehow — from the neat
Words to a hasty scrawl lower down the page.

A fearful left arm hides from sight
Thoughts that the other hand's been forced to write.

Count up the lines remaining blank
Until a side's been covered. Thank
Goodness there's no English homework set tonight!

Testing, Testing 123 Testing

You sit with paper blank
And wonder what to write.
The minutes tick,
The paper is still white.
Your head is full of thoughts
But none are right
To fill the lines
That flicker in your sight
And fade. Outside, the light
Is dimming too; perhaps some rain
Will come, or else the night.

And still the paper's blank:
You wonder what to write . . .

With no expression,
A netless tightropewalker:
He began the test.

Jabbermockery

Twas Thursday and the bottom set
Did gyre and gimble in the gym.
All mimsy was Miss Borogrove
And the Head of Maths was grim.

Beware the Mathematix, my friend!
His sums that snarl, his coordinates that catch!
Beware the Deputy-Bird, and shun
The evil Earring-Snatch!

She took her ballpoint pen in hand:
Longtime the problem's end she sought —
So rested she by the lavatory
And sat a while in thought.

And as in toughish thought she sat,
The Mathematix with eyes of flame
Came calculating through the cloakroom doors
And subtracted as he came!

She thought real fast as he went past;
The well-placed soap went slickersmack!
She left him stunned and with the sums
She went galumphing back.

And hast thou got the answers, Jackie?
Come to our desk, beamed idle boys,
Oh, frabjous day! Quelle heure! Calais!
They chortled in their joy.

Twas Thursday and the bottom set
Did gyre and gimble in the gym.
All mimsy was Miss Borogrove
And the Head of Maths was **grim.**

Ten Little Schoolchildren

10 little schoolchildren
standing in a line
one opened her mouth too far
and then there were 9

9 little schoolchildren
trying not to be late
one missed the school bus
then there were 8

8 little schoolchildren
in the second eleven
one twisted an ankle
and then there were 7

7 little schoolchildren
trying out some tricks
one went a bit too far
then there were 6

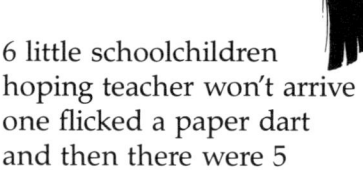

6 little schoolchildren
hoping teacher won't arrive
one flicked a paper dart
and then there were 5

5 little schoolchildren
standing by the door
one tripped the teacher up
and then there were 4

4 little schoolchildren
longing for their tea
one was kept in after school
and then there were 3

3 little schoolchildren
lurking by the loo
teacher saw a puff of smoke
then there were 2

2 little schoolchildren
think that fights are fun
one got a bloody nose
and then there was 1

1 little schoolchild
playing in the sun
whistle blew, buzzer went,
then there were none!

Exploding Heads (2)

I was hanging from the wall bars
In my customary way
When in came Mrs Packer
Like a pup about to play.

"You mustn't hang like that" she cried
"You're not a bat, you know, (I knew)
The blood'll rush down to your head
And then it will explode."

Ye Gods! I thought. I closed my eyes.
My head felt full and tight.
It would only need a tiny move
To set it off like dynamite!

The shock has really scared me.
Now on the bars I never hang
And I try to keep on lying down
To stop my feet from going bang.

The Head Boy's Refrain

No one wanted to be there
Save the Head *(wise man — or fool?)*
And those parents of pupils with prizes
On prize-getting day at school.

All were tired of the clapping,
Everyone sick of the listening.
At the back some heads were napping;
On the platform the faces were glistening.

Then the Head Boy, all proper and neat
By the mike made a noise rude and so loud
That the audience's jaws hit their feet
And the eyes of the parents so proud

Grew wide with the shock and dismay.
While he rushed from the Hall, rather red,
The clapping hands halted half way
As if clasping at cats that had fled . . .

Then at the back the smiles sprouted
And the smiles grew into great grins
And the grins developed into titters
— And then the laughter begins!

THE EVENING SHIFT

What Did You Do at School Today, Dear?

Copy the diagram on page 53
I copied it down with ruler and neatness
Though it didn't mean much at all to me . . .
. . . unlike
    A diagram of a Kawasaki
    A diagram of the girl across the row
    A diagram of the Head
       showing the holes where the bolts go.

Make notes on paragraphs 1 to 10
I copied every other sentence
Changed a few words, and then . . .
. . . made
    Notes on a twelve string guitar
    Notes on my mum's Moog synthesizer
    Notes on the girl across the avenue
       closely observed but none the wiser.

Questions 1 to 5 plus number 8.
Write your homework in the back of your book.
Hand in tomorrow. I don't want any in late. . .
. . . Ahhh
    Homework on the bus to school
    Homework while the twins are crying
    Homework with the girl across the room —
       she knows when to hand it in.

The Evening Shift

Sir, down there the telly's on
Can't concentrate
And it's bad for you, I'm told.
Upstairs is quiet and cold:
Can't think or write.
The kitchen's warm
But Mum will pester me all night
And make me do the washing up.

Shall I stand in the hall
And write on the wall
Or lie in the bath?
(Sir, it might not be correct
But at least it's clean . . .)

Don't worry, Sir, I'll manage
Even if I have to sit
On the lavatory seat
And balance my book on my knees;
It's not too much to please, Sir.

Even though the door
Was hammered to shreds
By brothers and mothers and Uncle Teds
Shouting, **How long are you going to be!?**

Only two more sentences to go!
You what!
Nothing, Uncle Ted; I won't be long.
Forgive me, Sir, if the spelling is all wrong.

The Song of the Homeworkers

*To be read or chanted with
increasing velocity*

Homework moanwork
Cross it out and groanwork
Homework neatwork
Keeps you off the streetwork
Homework moanwork
Cross it out and groanwork
Homework roughwork
When you've had enoughwork
Homework moanwork
Cross it out and groanwork
Homework dronework
Do it on your ownwork
Homework moanwork
Cross it out and groanwork
Homework gloomwork
Gaze around the roomwork
Homework moanwork
Cross it out and groanwork
Homework guesswork
Book is in a messwork
Homework moanwork
Cross it out and groanwork
Homework rushwork
Do it on the buswork
Homework moanwork
Cross it out and groanwork
Homework hatework
Hand your book in latework
Homework moanwork
Cross it out and groan **groan GROANWORK!**

Swap? Sell? Small Ads Sell Fast

1950 Dad. Good runner; needs one or
Two repairs; a few grey hairs but
Nothing a respray couldn't fix.
Would like a 1966 five speed turbo
In exchange: something in the sporty
Twin-carb range.

1920s Granny. Not many like this
In such clean and rust free state.
You must stop by to view! All chrome
As new, original fascia retained
Upholstery unstained. Passed MOT
Last week: will only swap for some-
Thing quite unique.

1986 low mileage Brother. As eco-
Nomical as any other. Must mention
Does need some attention. Stream-
Lined, rear spoiler. Runs on milk,
Baby oil and gripe water. Serviced;
Needs rear wash/wipe. Only one
Owner; not yet run in. Will swap
For anything.

Standing On My Head

My dad came into my room
which I share with my bed
and my brother
and asked in a voice calm
with long years of knowing me
why I was standing on my head on my bed.
I'm standing on my head on my bed
I said
So that when I fall from aloft
the fall will be soft.
But, said my dad,
Is that the best way
to do your homework, my lad?
Ah, but it's History, Dad,
and I need to think.
Oh, that's different, he said
and he left — with a wink.

Plug Her In
or
How to Deal With an Almost Adult Sister

At nine o'clock they leave:
Look after your brother;
Don't let him go out
In this cold and nasty weather.
She smiles
But I am not deceived,
Oh no I'm not:
My older sister
Is my one BIG
Weak spot!

So   I . . .
     Sit her in
     Her favourite place:
     In front of a mirror
     Staring at her face.
And I . . .
     Put a wad of spearmint
     In her everchewing mouth;
     Just chew and I
     I say — but
     She doesn't get the pun;
     Sometimes I think
     I'm the only one
     With a sense of humour
     In the human race.

Then I . . .
>Open this week's mag
>At the fashion page:
>*Black stripes* it squeaks
>*Are all the rage!*
>(Suit her really well,
>Especially down her cheeks.)

She's got . . .
>Lipstick in one hand
>And in the other a full
>Tube of some
>Revolting stuff
>She squeezes on her hair . . .
>Then, to crown it all
>I fit her personal stereo
>Like earmuffs
>Round her skull.

And now . . .
>the clear instructions
>Of my mum
>Are fading in her brain
>Like the flavour
>Of the gum . . .

Yes, I plugged my sister in
And went, rejoicing, out.
And now it's half past one —

I wonder if she's noticed
That I've gone?

Younger Brother

He collects bottle tops,
Toilet roll holders,
Dead insects,
Bits of rock and stones
Of interesting shape or colour,
Half made models,
Stickers, badges, pencils,
Feathers, germinating seeds,
Used socks (under the bed),
Broken saucers that he never mends,
Torch batteries, glass marbles,
Oh — and friends.

Alone in the House

I like being left alone
When everyone's gone out.
I change from Channel 1 to 3
And from 3 to 4 to 2,
I play the music centre
As loud as it will go,
I call up Dial-a-Recipe
And talk back to the voice,
Search the fridge and larder
For leftover luxuries,
Put pickled onions and bananas
In my giant sandwiches,
I crunch the solid icy peas
Straight from the freezer tray
And write notes to our milkman
'Three hundred pints today'.
I creep round in the darkness
Pretending I'm a burglar or a cat,
I slither head first down the stairs
In my brother's sleeping bag
And I read the books my sister
Keeps hidden from my dad.
Then . . .
I sit down with my sandwich
In my father's favourite chair
Put my feet up on the table
And feel glad that they're not there
. . . once in a while.

DREAMS AND MEMORIES

I Dreamt I Took Over My Secondary School

I dreamt I took over my secondary school:
Sacked the Headmaster for breaking the rules,
Kept the Teachers outside during break in the cold
And took all their cigarettes: *You're really too old
To be smoking — haven't you learnt **yet**,* I said.
Learn to say no; you're too easily led!
I told them to stop talking and messing about,
*The staff room's a cess pit. Get it cleaned out!
And, Deputy, don't drive that car like a bat out of hell —
Wait in the car park till the end-of-school bell.*
I called in the matron and checked them for nits,
Tested their eyes and then tested their wits.
Gave the staff an IQ test, kept them in after school;
Made them read out their answers so they'd each feel a fool.
I sent several home to change shirts or their ties
Or put on dull dresses of more suitable size.
I gave lots of homework, which I didn't explain —
They put up their hands and asked questions in vain.
You should have been listening, I said with a smile;
Hand in tomorrow. Now line up in single file!
I ignored their excuses that they had to go out,
Your work must come first! I said with a shout.
*Reports will be issued at the end of the term —
If you've not shown improvement, I'll have to be firm:
It may be the thumbscrews, it may be the rack . . .
I'm going to wake up now . . . but I'll be back!*

A Glimpse

I got a glimpse of Granny
Staring at the setting sun;
How do I know it's Granny
When she looks so very young?

I got a glimpse of Granny
Standing on the Sea-front Walk
And by her side a gentleman;
They stood but did not talk.

I got a glimpse of Granny
Walking a black pram.
Why does that simple picture
Make me wonder who I am?

I got a glimpse of Granny
And the letter in her hand;
Was it read or was it sealed
As she walked along the sand?

I got a glimpse of Granny;
She was staring out to sea.
When she looked down at the photograph
Did she get a glimpse of me?

Deferred Gratifications

They call it D G
In books about society
That sixth formers carry
And college people read.
It means putting off
Enjoying things till later . . .
Like getting down to your homework
Instead of the disco
So you'll pass your exams
And then you'll be glad
Won't you?
(*Be able to count the dole*
And spell unemployed.)
Like working and saving
Instead of going out raving
So you'll be able to
Enjoy your retirement
(*Just don't die too soon!*)
Deferred Gratifications.
None of my friends
Seem to believe in it . . .
Except my girlfriend.

Caught Short, A Dream

The motor mower (*thuggety thug*) outside the classroom
Growing louder each time (*THUGGETY THUG*) something's said
And behind it, perched on a roller (*thuggety thug*) like a jelly
Slipped from its mould, a fat groundsman with a belly
Hanging over the shorn grass
Is (*thuggety thuggery*) about to pass
Into some sort of sagging slumber
(*THUGetty THug*) catching a number
Of white stick insect cricketers unawares . . .
        A sudden slump
Of belly onto throttle and a *THUGGETTY THUGG*
Through the lot — wicket, ball,
Batsman, bat, pads and all.
Together with two men (*thuggety blug*)
From the slips, their sliced remains,
Like diced white beans, disappearing underneath
More flying cuttings (*thmuggety thmug*): a sort of wreath . . .
        And back inside
The classroom, we watch enthralled
As the umpire, rightly, signals *No Ball*;
        We all applaud.

The Jungle Sale . . . Another Dream

Let's go to the Jungle Sale
Buy an ant or a great white whale
What a bungle,
You don't get whales in the jungle!
But anyway, we went
Into the giant marquee tent
And Debbie bought a second hand leopard
With rather faded spots
And lots
Of lovely fleas
(*No extra charge for these*).
John bought a boa constrictor
With her elastic a little bit worn
And Betty got a bat
Very black
But slightly torn.
Jim found a small, damp
Turtle with a touch of cramp
And Susan got a centipede
Which limped,
A yellowhammer with a stammer
And a shrimp that was afraid of the sea.
Kalima came home
With a very friendly pelican
Which had a leak
In its beak
And a very curious disease.
You can imagine how their mums and dads
Were pleased!
Bet you wish you'd gone
To the:

Roll up, Roll up!
One and all!
Never Fail
Church Bizarre
And one and only Jungle Sale!

Embarrassing Memories from the Playground

I remember
in the playground
being called
the teacher's pet
and what I minded
most
was that the teacher
might have heard
and be upset.

I remember
in the playground
playing rounders,
daydreaming on the base
because the girl
that I fancied
most
in all the school
was playing too . . .
and, came the time to run,
I forgot
and she was out!
She shouted at me
and I felt a fool.

I remember
in the playground
fighting that boy
with the green cord jacket
and what surprised me
most
was that I wasn't so bad at it
after all, though
the awkward thing
was knowing what to do
when you'd finished . . .
did you just get up and go?

Sad I Ams

I am
    the ring
    from an empty Cola can
    the scrapings
    from an unwashed porridge pan
    the severed arm
    of last year's Action Man.

I am
    the envelope
    on which the gum is gone
    the sellotape
    where you can't find the end
    the toothless stapler, springless bulldog clip
    the dried up liquid paper
    that mars instead of mends
    the stamped addressed reply
    that you forgot
    to send.

I am
    the battery in which no charge is left
    the starter motor which remains inert
    the tyre on which the tread is worn
    the sparking plug which shows no sign of
    spark
    the carburettor choked by bits of dirt
    the chromium trim from which the shine has
    gone.

I am
    a garden
    overgrown with weeds
    a library book
    that no one ever reads
    a stray
    which no one thinks to feed
    the piece of good advice
    which no one seems to need.

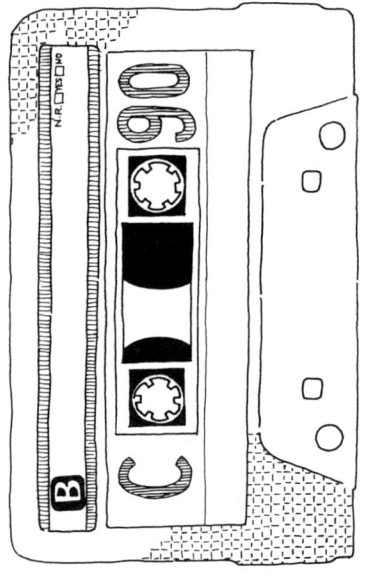

One day I hope
You'll want to go
FAST FORWARD ▶▶
Till then,
PAUSE ∥
& don't
EJECT me ⏏

Fragments Overheard
Villanelle

Our growing up's a time of hearing words
Intended for some other ears instead,
And knowledge comes from fragments overheard.

The feelings we thought funny or absurd
We hear round doors or while tucked into bed:
Our growing up's a time of hearing words

And making out that nothing has occurred —
That we didn't understand the things they said;
But knowledge comes from fragments overheard.

Do we reveal or not that we have heard
The news that Auntie's pregnant, Grandad's dead?
Our growing up's a time of hearing words

And knowing half the meanings. Nothing stirred.
And then a chair scraped back. I rose and fled:
Our growing up's a time of hearing words,
And knowledge comes from fragments overheard . . .

ESCAPE

Don't Pick It!

In the welly woolly winter
I picked the brussel sprouts
Threw them all about the garden
Like huge frozen drops
Of snot, I'd shout —
    And didn't me mum
    Fetch me a huge and frozen clout!
    (*She rearranged my face*)

In the spry and nippy spring
I picked the daffodils
Tied them up with string
A bunch of precious yellow
For me mum . . .
    But Dad
    Made my precious backside sting!
    (*Said it was a dreadful waste*)

In the swarmy swimming summer
Off the ageing garden shed
I picked the peely paint
And filled in all the gaps
With fluorescent day-glo felt-tip red!
    And then got sent to bed!
    (*It wasn't to everybody's taste*)

In the awful gloomy autumn
I'm not even gonna
Pick my
Nose.

On Yer Bike

Down the road
  Between the cars
    Sudden beeping
      Screeching tyres

Turning tumbling

        over
         handlebars!

  Stars!
    Stars!
Did I see stars?

      Planets!

    Moons!

        Jupiter!

            Mars!

Then . . .
    . . . dimly . . .
        . . . the bars
of hospital beds . . .
Head a mixture
        Of blues and reds
    And white where bandages

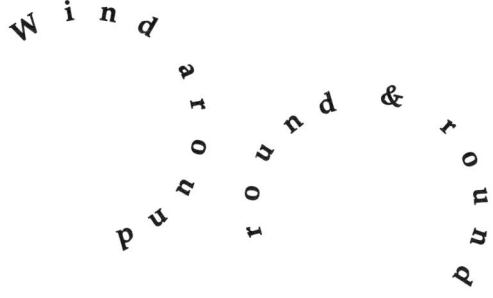

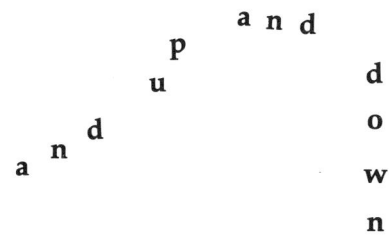

I can hardly breathe
        For cotton gauze,
    My hands have turned

    Into soft white paws. . .

But every passing nurse assures
Me I'll be fine
    And back on my bike
        In next to no time,
            Wheeling along
                Just as I like!

Bike?
    Bike!
        I blink through the pain
        I think they must think
        I'm insane!
        Do they think the shock
        Has blocked my brain?
        You'll not get me
        On that
            mad
                machine
                    again!

The Power of Positive Thinking

It was that snowy January
Me mam sent me round
To see if our nan
Wanted owt from the shops . . .

    I hoped she wouldn't be in
(*Did I think she'd be out making snowmen?*)
    I hoped she'd not answer the door
(*Fearing I was the Mad Axeman*)
    I hoped she wouldn't want anything
(*Having got in stocks of rice pudding and
kippers till spring*)
    But — she was at home
        — was really glad I had come
        — and shopping? There certainly was
        some!

    I hoped she wouldn't want much
(*Just a packet of tea and a sprout*)
    I hoped she'd not give me the flowery bag
(*Too big to hide up my jumper*)
    I hoped I wouldn't meet someone I knew
(*If only the blizzard would break!*)
    But — a list a mile long
        — a bag with pink roses sewn on
        — and there, at the corner, stood John.

Oh no!

I gave up hoping
Tried positive thinking.
Hi John — give us a hand.
I'm getting some stuff for me nan.

It was him who looked sheepish
Him who looked bad
As he ummed and he ahhed
And he said,

Well, I would if I could
But I'm late.
I'm sorry, er,
See you 'round, mate.
I nodded with style
And I laughed to myself
As I strode round the shops
With a smile.

Theatre Trip

Sir sat at the back
In his hat and his mac
To prevent any likely mayhem;
Samantha and Heather
Sat close together
But he wasn't thinking of **them**.

His eyes were on Johnny
Who thinks he's real funny
A boy with a *lively* expression;
But the way that he speaks
And his white pasty cheeks
Are enough to give any teacher depression.

When we got to the place
The red carpet was ace
And the stairs were as wide as a street;
The seats were so high
You felt you might fly
Though there was no room to stick out your feet.

We're allowed to chew sweets
Except, *Under the seats*
No traces of gum must be found . . .
And if you must eat
Crisps, let me repeat:
Consume them without any sound!

There were whistles and shouts
When the house lights went out
Cos it seemed we'd been waiting an age;

But the costumes and noises
Made us lower our voices
As the actors stepped onto the stage.

There was smoke coloured green
From a clever machine
And a bang that made eyeballs pop out;
I shot up where I sat
My ice cream went splat
And even Miss Scott gave a shout!

There were dragons and witches
And blokes without britches
So some kids thought it too young;
But when villains got nabbed
And the baddies were stabbed
We cheered from the depths of our lungs.

Then Sir gave a stare
That John isn't there!
Now where can that idiot be?
Through all of Act Two
He looked through the loos
But abandoned his search in Act Three.

Miss Scott said, *Too bad.*
I've warned that young lad;
I'm not staying here for the night.
If he's not back at the end
He'll just have to fend
For himself — serves him right!

Then the audience cheered;
Sharon said, *He's appeared!*
As a figure lurched into the limelight;
He ran off pretty fast
As one of the cast
Seemed determined to give him stage fright.

Lost me way, he said after
As he grinned through the laughter
And avoided Sir's murderous glances;
*I didn't get far
But I **could** be a star:
And a star must be prepared to take chances!*

He tried to look cool
On the way back to school
But some girls know just how to be cruel;
Don't get big ideas
Said Jane loud in his ears
*The only part **you'll** act is the **fool!***

Leaving School Blues

There was a time when I was at school
Not keepin, not breakin, just mindin the rules,
Just sittin down and starin ahead
Wonderin why I'd got out of bed;
Saw plenty of blackboards, plenty of books,
Went out of my way to get a good look —
Out the window . . .

Same walls, same rooms, same corridors,
Same old ceilins, same old floors;
Thought of the day when freedom would come,
Freedom from Dad, freedom from Mum,
Freedom from school . . .

Left that buildin — fast — soon as I could;
Didn't have anythin folks said I should:
Didn't bother much about qualifications,
Grandad said you get a proper education
Out in the *real* world . . .
                                        . . . sure was right . . .

Got a job in an office, nine till five,
Earned enough to keep alive,
Carried messages, said yes and no,
Obeyed instructions (*advice you know*)
Saw the same old faces day after day,
Same routine: so what do you say?
Pretty boring . . .

Left the office for wider skies,
Joined a factory makin pies;
Machine wheels turned and so did I
Thought one day I'd *look* like a pie:
Watch out! . . . Don't eat me . . .

Gotta clock in and gotta clock out,
Five minutes late and some gaffer'll shout;
But I got promotion in my very second week:
For a kid like me, that's quite a break . . .
Pulling three leavers — instead of two!
Wow . . . some high flier . . .

Same old faces, same old rhymes,
Left the works for more excitin times;
Get away from routine, rules and things,
Get some experience and try my wings!
. . . Joined the army . . .

So much excitement, I couldn't wait,
Polishin coal and standin straight,
Stood to attention twenty times a day;
It's a man's life in the army, so they say.
That's called . . . propaganda . . .

They cut my hair and gave me boots,
Cleaned me up from twigs to roots,
Sent me out Northern Ireland way,
Said to me I'd enjoy my stay . . .
. . . While it lasted . . .

★ ★ ★

That used to be the very last verse
Cos I thought things couldn't get no worse:
However hard it rains, you don't get wetter —
Told my brother and sister it could only
get better . . .
    I was na. . .ive . . .

Time went by and dole queues grew;
They soon learnt what everyone knew;
They had their education, had their fling,
They didn't have jobs — but got the next
best thing . . .
    You guessed it . . . Y.T.Ssed it . . .

Things aren't as bad as they seem, you know.
Create the wealth and the jobs will grow.
Don't sit around on your fat backside —
Get on your bike and take a ride . . .
    To High Wycombe . . .? Tunbridge Wells . . . ?
    Taiwan . . .?

Still waitin for the turn of the tide
Still waitin for a bike to ride!
They say, *See light at the end of the tunnel soon!*
Yeah . . . we're all lookin for a nice blue moon . . .
    Sure is a long tunnel . . .

IDEAS FOR WRITING

IDEAS FOR WRITING

Introduction	109
The Raid of the Head-Bangers	110
Bell Rings	111
Guarantee and E322	112
Paper Round	113
Junk Mail	114
Head Cold	116
Chemistry/Istri/Art/English	117
If I Was a Frog	117
The Summons	119
Duet	120
Mr Taylor's All Right/Jane Johnson	121
I Really Tried	121
Teacher Giving Orders	122
New Teacher — Old Class	123
Jabbermockery	126
Ten Little Schoolchildren	129
What Did You Do at School Today?	130
Evening Shift and	132
The Song of the Homeworkers	
Swap? Sell? Small Ads Sell Fast	133
Younger Brother/Older Sister	134
I Dreamt I Took Over My Secondary School	135
Caught Short/Jungle Sale	
Sad I Ams	135
Fragments Overheard	137
Haiku	138
Conversation Poems	140
Shared Poems	142

INTRODUCTION

This section contains ideas which may help you to write poems of your own. They are suggestions, or opportunities. If you want to alter or adapt the ideas, feel free.

You will find that a lot of the suggestions involve using a pattern for your writing. I think it's helpful to have a pattern or a form to work to as long as it doesn't become the be-all and end-all.

Silly rhymes and *di-dum-di-dum-di-dum* rhythms are bound to occur. Don't worry. Once you've learned to spot them you will start to be able to avoid them. Give yourself time. Don't expect instant results. Even the simplest poem in the collection has been altered lots of times (*believe it or not*) until I was satisfied with it. Only rarely does the *right* version come out first time.

THE RAID OF THE HEAD-BANGERS

When you've got a headache it isn't hard to imagine that your head is full of vandalising gremlins. Think of your own experience of headaches — or any other pain from toothache to appendicitis — and write about it in a similar way. No two people have quite the same image of what's causing the pain — it could be anything from razortoothed ferrets to soldier ants armed with red-hot chisels.

BELL RINGS

Write a machine poem on your own day or anyone else's day that you know or can imagine — in a factory, an office, at home . . .

BELL RINGS . . . BUZZER GOES . . . CLOCK TICKS . . . WATCH BEEPS

You could turn your poem or the original poem into a simple strip cartoon.

Turn to page 90 and look at the cassette picture poem. Use another machine or part of a machine to describe how you feel . . . a kitchen mixer . . . a computer . . . a spark plug . . . ?

If you haven't come across it before, you might want to look up a poem along similar lines, called the *Computer's First Christmas Card,* by Edwin Morgan.

GUARANTEE and E322

The first verse of *Guarantee* is taken directly from the side of a *Sugar Puffs* packet and the description of ingredients in *E322* is taken more or less directly from the wrapper of a chocolate (or chocolate flavoured) biscuit whose name I have forgotten. The sign *OAPS 20% Off* which is used elsewhere in this book also really exists. Signs, adverts, newspaper headlines — all sorts of things can provide you with ideas for writing. By altering and adapting you can often make something quite amusing or unusual from something which at first looked very ordinary.

PAPER ROUND

Any job you do, from a paper round to cleaning out the hamster cage, can provide you with the ideas you need for writing. *Paper Round* uses *One, Two, Buckle My Shoe* as a basic framework. Such a framework can help in this as in any other poem but it isn't essential.

On similar lines you could use *The Twelve Days of Christmas* as a framework for something:

> *On the first day of the holidays*
> *My father made me clean*
> *A dirty car in the driveway.*
> *On the second day of the holidays*
> *My father made me clean*
> *Two muddy boots*
> *And a dirty car in the driveway . . .*
>   and see how far you get!

JUNK MAIL

Junk Mail, like several other poems in this book, is written as a song. What's the difference? To me, the difference is that I can hear the words being sung as I write them. If you want your writing to have a definite rhythm or beat to it, this can help. When you try to sing it you'll soon know if you got it wrong, and where!

The beat I heard in my head for *Junk Mail* was very simple:

it flaps through-the-door looking nice-&-fat

Some lines have extra syllables which affect the rhythm slightly but the *da-da-dum* at the end of each line remains steady. The rhythm I had in mind for the last three lines of the chorus was very jerky and was intended to be shouted rather than sung!

Read other poems from this and different poetry books and find some which could be songs. Write down a rough beat for them — and a melody too, if you can. Don't worry about exact musical notation.

Try adding a verse of your own to this or any other song — just to see if you've got the basic idea. It doesn't matter at this stage if the words don't make complete sense . . . Now you're ready to write your own song.

For me, the words come first. Usually I get a couple of lines in my mind which spark off two or three ways of being sung. I decide on one and then the rest of the song/poem follows. Not being particularly musical, my tunes are usually simple and fairly repetitive — but you don't know what you can do till you try. This is another area where you can work in pairs: one of you may be able to put the other's words to music!

HEAD COLD

Poems can be written about very very simple and everyday things. There's this one about getting your brain working and elsewhere there are poems about headaches, chocolate biscuits, doing homework, the dog's name — all from a personal point of view.
Read *Head Cold* and *The Raid of the Head-Bangers* and write your feelings about, say, getting up in the morning, getting a cold, sneezing . . .

CHEMISTRY/ISTRI/ART/ENGLISH

School subjects are a good source of material for writing, in praise or in criticism. The four poems take very different approaches. In *Chemistry* the writer compares him/herself to a particular chemical. You could perhaps imagine yourself having something in common with something used or discussed in one of your lessons?

In *Istri* the writer mainly delights in strings of good-sounding names. You could either add some lines to the ones already there or try a totally new version — using new subject areas . . .
Permanganate . . . Dichromate . . . perhaps?

IF I WAS A FROG

You might be all sorts of things, other than a pupil. Use the same pattern as *If I Was a Frog* and write a similar poem:

If I was an orang-utan, I'd _____

If I was a boa constrictor, I'd _____

If I was a _____

(and so on)
But as I'm a _____

You could be things other than animals . . .
If I was a ballpoint pen
I'd retract.

Trace the desk outline onto your paper and draw on your own creature to illustrate your poem.

THE SUMMONS

When you are asked to see a teacher, especially a Head Teacher, a Deputy Head, a Head of Year or a Head of House, your first reaction is usually, *What have I done?* Which really means, *What have I done wrong that they've found out about?*

Choose the name of a particular teacher in your school to whom you would not like to be called and use it in the first line of a poem:

Mr
*Mrs*_____*called my name*
Miss
Ms

                  or

Mr
Mrs _____*sent for me*
Miss
Ms

Make a list of all the things you could have done wrong but haven't . . .

I haven't left my kit behind
I didn't run along the corridor
I wasn't late for registration . . .

You could end it something like this:

BUT _____
And **that's** *what they found out about!*

DUET

Read the poem through with one voice taking the *heroic* lines and another voice reading the *ordinary* lines.

The pattern of this poem is quite east to imitate. You can tell a story in a similar way: seeing it through two different pairs of eyes, two different points of view. It need not be *heroic* and *ordinary*, it could be *science fiction* and *ordinary* or *gangster* and *ordinary*. There are many possibilities.

The sinister dark-suited guy stormed in
   Dad came home late

It might work with a combination of *science fiction* and *heroic* etc — but I've never tried it and I think the down to earth lines are needed in order to create the anticlimax which creates the humour.

This type of poem looks as if it would work well written in pairs. In fact, it's quite difficult to do that way because the writer of the *ordinary* lines needs to know what's going on in the mind of the first writer. However, if you like working in pairs and have a partner you work well with, it's worth trying.

MR TAYLOR'S ALL RIGHT/JANE JOHNSON

These poems are about fairly ordinary people. (*You can't get much more humdrum than poor Jane.*) They show that there's something to be said about **anyone** if you want to. It does help to observe the person and make some notes before you start — unless you've got a good memory — but try not to let them see you, it will make them very nervous. Choose a victim and have a go!

I REALLY TRIED

Write a list of excuses, starting with believable ones and ending up with incredible ones. This can be done individually, as a group or as a class.

I couldn't do my homework
Because . . .

I forgot to feed the cat
Because . . .

I can't pay back that 50p
Because . . .

I can't . . .
Because . . .

Think of other phrases that are often used:

You should have thought of that before!
How many times have you been told?
Just wait till I get you home!
and so on . . .

Choose such a phrase and use it as the first or last line of a number of verses.

TEACHER GIVING ORDERS

Perhaps you would like to place an order — for teachers, friends or relatives?

I'd like a set of teachers
No one very strict
One or two with _____
And _____

Half a dozen friends, please,
All loyal to the core,

_____
_____

Some fresh grown aunts and uncles
And perhaps a cousin, too,

_____
_____

NEW TEACHER — OLD CLASS

I suppose this comes close to being what is called concrete poetry. The best known examples of concrete poetry are *calligrams*. A calligram is really just a poem written in the shape of something, like this:

A BUTTERFLY IS A TINY SUNBEAM, AN EXPLOSION OF LIGHT, A MINUTE WATERFALL OF AIRBORNE COLOURS. TO CATCH IT IS TO CATCH A RAINBOW IN THE PALM OF THE HAND, A WISP OF AIR, ETERNAL, BEAUTIFUL, AND FREE. TRULY A GIFT OF GOD.

Calligram or concrete, this kind of poetry achieves its effects by the way it arranges the words on the page. In *New Teacher Old Class* the words are arranged in three *verses* but each verse is meant to look something like a classroom — teacher in front, pupils arranged in rows. Take a look also at *On Yer Bike* where there are a couple of examples within the poem.

Sometimes this kind of thing is a way of disguising not very good writing! *My desk is made of wood and stands on four legs. It's quite flat* is not made into a better poem by being written:

```
MY DESK IS MADE IT'S
 OF WOOD AND STANDS ON
  FOUR  LEGS        FLAT.  QUITE
```

However, if you've written a short poem which would suit this kind of presentation, make the best of it. Plan its layout carefully, working out how the words should be arranged to look best.

 If you're setting out to write a poem which could then be presented as a calligram, start with some observation. Observe your cat/budgie/stick insect/cactus and make a note of everything you see, hear, smell, feel (*or taste, if appropriate — though I don't think it's worth licking the cactus or eating the budgie just for the sake of a poem*). Then you can pick out the parts which you (*or others*) like best and use them for your poem. For example, a 14 year old wrote:

My cat is as vain as a film star or a queen like Cleopatra. She purrs like she has an engine deep down in her throat or her chest and her evil green eyes shine in her face like emeralds. She miaows pathetically and gets ignored or fed. But later behind her half-closed eyelids she dribbles in contentment. She sleeps all day, lazy as a cow but I suppose she's as gentle and as gracious as a ballerina when she wants to be. When she walks along the wall it's as if she's a tightrope walker on padded paws. When she's asleep she's just like any other furry fat cat.

Her final version went like this:

Smug and vain like
Cleopatra,
Deep in her throat her
Engine purrs and
Evil green eyes shine
Like emeralds.
Behind half-closed
Eyelids,
Dribbling in contentment
Lazy as a cow —
But gentle and gracious
Like a ballerina:
She is a tightrope walker
On padded paws.

JABBERMOCKERY

This is a parody of the original poem by **Lewis Carroll** which you've probably heard. In case you haven't, there's a copy of it at the end of this section. By comparing the two poems you will see what a parody is — a kind of imitation which keeps enough of the original in it for it to be clear that it *is* a copy and not something totally fresh. Parodies are usually written to send up or make fun of the original, though in the case of *Jabbermockery* this wasn't the intention.
Lewis Carroll himself wrote a parody of the well-known nursery rhyme:

> *Twinkle twinkle little star*
> *How I wonder what you are*
> *Up above the world so high*
> *Like a diamond in the sky.*

His version went like this:

> *Twinkle twinkle little bat*
> *How I wonder what you're at*
> *Up above the world you fly*
> *Like a tea-tray in the sky.*

A famous poem by **Coleridge** begins:

> *In Xanadu did Kubla Khan*
> *A stately pleasure dome decree:*
> *Where Alph, the sacred river, ran*
> *Through caverns measureless to man*
> *Down to a sunless sea.*

A parody of this by **B. A. Phythian** goes:

> *In Bakerloo did Aly Khan*
> *A stately Hippodrome decree:*
> *Where Alf, the bread delivery man,*
> *Brought crumpets in his horse drawn van*
> *Down to the A.B.C*

Try your hand at some parodies of nursery rhymes or other poems. The better known the original, the better the parody — a parody of an unknown poem is pretty pointless!

The Tyger, by **William Blake**; *Night Mail,* by **W. H. Auden** or *Daffodils* by **William Wordsworth** might be worth trying.

> *Roger, Roger, turning right*
> *In the back-streets of the night*
> *What sharp-seeing driver's eye*
> *Detects the rear light on your bike?*

> *This is the junk-mail*
> *Crossing the doormat*
> *Bringing the _____*
> *And the _____*

Jabberwocky

'Twas brillig, and the slithy toves
  Did gyre and gimble in the wabe;
All mimsy were the borogroves
  And the mome raths outgrabe.

'Beware the Jabberwock, my son!
  The jaws that bite, the claws that catch!
Beware the Jubjub bird, and shun
  The frumious Bandersnatch!'

He took his vorpal sword in hand:
  Long time the manxome foe he sought -
So rested he by the Tumtum tree,
  And stood awhile in thought.

And as in uffish thought he stood,
  The Jabberwock, with eyes of flame,
Came whiffling through the tulgey wood,
  And burbled as it came!

One, two! One, two! And through and through
  The vorpal blade went snicker-snack!
He left it dead, and with its head
  He went galumphing back.

'And hast thou slain the Jabberwock?
  Come to my arms, my beamish boy!
O frabjous day! Callooh! Callay!'
  He chortled in his joy.

'Twas brillig, and the slithy toves
  Did gyre and gimble in the wabe;
All mimsy were the borogoves,
  And the mome raths outgrabe.

Lewis Carroll

TEN LITTLE SCHOOLCHILDREN

This is an easy and satisfying pattern to use. The only thing you have to remember is that you have to rhyme with all the numbers up to nine. Luckily, they are all very easy to rhyme apart from seven. Any ideas apart from eleven and heaven? Devon, of course, but how much use if *that* going to be?

Choose your own grouping . . .

10 little gymnasts
Leaping _____
*One leapt*_____
And then there were nine

10 little disco-dancers
10 little dinner ladies
10 little dragons
10 rusty mini-vans
10 little budgerigars

WHAT DID YOU DO AT SCHOOL TODAY?

Well? You must have done *something!*
Pick out four or five things you did or which were said or that you saw someone else do and write them as short paragraphs.

Now: keep only the precise details in what you have written and cross out everything else.

The boy across the aisle from me was (writing his history notes) and his pen which was a (fountain pen slipped out of his fingers) and dropped on his book. The (ink splatted) out and made a mess over (the whole page.) When (Miss) found out she (called) him a clumsy clot) and (gave him three paper hankies.)

Write out what's left. Each paragraph becomes one verse. If you can find a way of ending each verse in a similar fashion, perhaps with a rhyme or a repeated phrase like *I'm glad it wasn't me* you may find you've made a pleasant little poem. At the very least you'll have an unusual record of one day in your life.

The boy across the aisle
Writing history notes –
Fountain pen slipped
From his fingers;
Ink splattered
Over the whole page.
Miss gave him
Three paper hankies
And called him a clumsy clot
(He said quietly, "I'm not.")

EVENING SHIFT AND THE SONG OF THE HOMEWORKERS

Add some more lines to *The Song of the Homeworkers.*

What rhythm would you use to chant it?

home-work, moan-work, cross it out and groan-work

A simple melody could be written for it . . .

home-work, moan-work, cross it out and groan-work

How about a song beginning:

Housework, grousework

_____

_____

Housework, grousework

_____

_____

And so on . . .

(It's worth a try — but it's harder than it looks.)

Write a poem — in any style — called *Homework at My House.*

SWAP? SELL? SMALL ADS SELL FAST

Anybody you'd like to sell or swap?
Advertise them!

YOUNGER BROTHER/OLDER SISTER

Think (*if you can bear it*) about a brother or a sister or a parent or anyone else you know well. Jot down in rough all the things you can think of to do with them — **especially their little habits:**

She leaves hairs in the plughole
He sings, We'll keep a welcome in the hillsides *while he's shaving*
He always pats his stomach after a meal
She always says be good *when she goes out*

Write the most interesting ones in a list and illustrate what you've written with little pictures or diagrams around the outside.

I DREAMT I TOOK OVER MY SECONDARY SCHOOL
CAUGHT SHORT/JUNGLE SALE

In a dream anything can happen. In these poems, especially the last one, the happenings are absurd. If you set out deliberately to write something that's absurd you have to be careful, or it is quite likely to end up by just being silly. Usually, it is the mixture of the ridiculous and the normal which makes things funny or appealing in some other way. For example, apart from the items on sale, the jumble/jungle sale is perfectly ordinary; apart from the cricketers being reduced to something like grass-high, all the other details in *Caught Short* are quite as they should be. So, if you want to write a poem that's a dream, now's your chance . . .

SAD I AMS

Try some of your own . . .

I am
    the empty paper cup

    the doorbell
___

    the light bulb
___

I am

_____
_____
_____
_____
_____
_____
_____
_____

Six to eight lines is a good length. It's often a good idea to write quite a lot more than you need and then pick out (*or get a friend to help you pick out*) the best ones.

I am
  the ace
  that won the tennis match
  the carnation
  selected for the bride's bouquet
  the _____

_____
_____
_____

FRAGMENTS OVERHEARD

This poem is written according to a particular pattern or form, which is called a *villanelle*. The first line and the third line are repeated at regular intervals and are put together as the final two lines. Apart from this difficulty, you only have two rhymes to work with so you have to choose words with care! It's not easy but you might want to try — and it doesn't matter if you don't get everything right. However, you will need **patience.**

Finding the right first line is often the key . . .

When I grew up I put away my childhood toys

sounds good — but does *toys* have enough variety of rhyme? *Boys, enjoys, annoys, destroys, employs, noise* . . . Perhaps. If you're not sure you can usually make a small alteration and keep the same sense:

When I grew up I put away my childhood things.

From then on it's a question of trying lines out, trying again, rethinking, leaving it for a day, moving lines around, going for a walk, having a new idea . . .

I tried to write this poem several times

might be a good line to start and end with.
Good Luck!

HAIKU

There are many other books that will tell you all about *Haiku* and how to write them. In terms of pattern, they are little poems of three lines, with 5 syllables in the first line, 7 in the second and 5 in the third line. There's only one (*apart from the one below*) in this book; see if you can find it.

A single comparison can form the basis of a very satisfying Haiku.
Begin with a random selection of comparisons:

A fat man is like . . .
The hawk circled like . . .
The skeleton rattled like . . .
She smiled like . . .
And so on
And on

When you have made a long list, choose (*or get a friend to choose*) two or three of the best. A thirteen year old chose:
The hawk circled like a carousel in the sky
and used it as the first and last line of a poem:

A carousel in the sky

———————————

The hawk circled.

She put in a second line so that the completed poem read:

On a carousel in the sky
Riding gently
The hawk circled.

It could equally have been:

Riding gently
On a carousel in the sky
The hawk circled.

But she preferred the first version

"But what about the five, seven and five syllables?" I said.
"It's all right as it is," she said.

She was right. If the pattern of your poem gets in the way of what you're writing — and you're happy with what you've written — ignore the pattern.

CONVERSATION POEMS

first writer   **second writer**

Hi Matt, how's you?

                                  Not bad, how's you?

I'm feeling glum

                                  Is it yer mum?

No, she's fine today

                                  Is yer dad away?

Yeah, for a week or two

                                  That why you're blue?

No, _____

                                  _____

_____

and so on

I think this is one kind of poem which needs to rhyme if it's going to work. It's up to the first writer to end his or her line with an easy rhyme — and after a few lines it might be fair to swap round so that someone else has the problem of finding the rhyme. You'll probably need several tries at this before getting anything which you think is worth keeping.

This can also be done as a game in which the second writer can challenge the first if he or she cannot think of a suitable rhyme. I suggest you swap round every four lines and agree beforehand whether to accept near rhymes.

E.g. *Hello Sue, how's tricks?*

My brother's sick

see also SHARED POEMS.

SHARED POEMS

These work best if there's a definite pattern to them, like a rhyme or an agreed number of syllables in each line. It is probably easier to work in pairs although threesomes do sometimes produce interesting results.

To begin with it's hard to keep such poems from becoming silly. After a few tries, though, it should be possible to write ten or twelve reasonably good lines. If you can agree beforehand on what your poem will be about, it will probably work better but be prepared to go along with spontaneous ideas. Don't interrupt the process in the middle just to tell the other writer that he or she is one syllable short in one of the lines. Wait till you agree that overall your poem is OK (*or brilliant*) and then you can go back, check on details and make improvements.

Trevor Millum has been teaching English in secondary schools for sixteen years, in Zambia, Singapore and England. He has been writing as long as he can remember and has published articles, poems and books including: *Images of Woman: Visual Communication in Advertising*, in 1975; *Exercises in African History*, in 1977 and *Traffic Island and Other Stories*, in 1984, based on his experiences in Asia.

He is currently Head of English at a comprehensive school in Humberside, and is editing a collection of short stories entitled *Pigs is Pigs*. He is also working on more short stories, poems and plays, and a novel for young people.